Fishing

Paul Mason

MACMILLAN
LIBRARY

First published in 2007 by
MACMILLAN EDUCATION AUSTRALIA PTY LTD
627 Chapel Street, South Yarra 3141

Visit our website at www.macmillan.com.au or go directly to www.macmillanlibrary.com.au
Associated companies and representatives throughout the world.

National Library of Australia
Cataloguing-in-Publication data

Mason, Paul, 1967– .
  Fishing.

  Includes index.
  For primary school aged children.
  ISBN 978 1 4202 0583 1 (hbk.).
  ISBN 1 4202 0583 8 (hbk.).

  1. Fishing. I. Title. (Series: Mason, Paul, 1967– .
  Recreational sports).

799.1

Edited by Vanessa Lanaway
Text and cover design by Pier Vido
Page layout by Pier Vido
Photo research by Naomi Parker
Illustrations by Boris Silvestri
Map on pp. 28–9 by Pier Vido

Printed in China

Acknowledgements
The author and the publisher are grateful to the following for permission to reproduce
copyright material:

Front cover photograph: Man fishing in a river, courtesy of Jordan Shaw/Istockphoto.

Photos courtesy of:
Stephen Frink/Corbis/Australian Picture Library, p. 20 (bottom); Stephen Booth, pp. 7
(bottom), 8, 24, 26; Anne Ackermann/Getty Images, p. 25; Magnus Fond/Getty Images, p. 30;
Johner/Getty Images, pp. 4, 21; Curtis Johnson/Getty Images, p. 7 (top); Mark Lewis/Getty
Images, pp. 22, 27; Ian Sanderson/Getty Images, p. 23 (top); Arthur Tilley/Getty Images,
p. 18; Melissa Carroll/Istockphoto, p. 6; Elaine Lanmon/Istockphoto, p. 13 (top); Courtnee
Mulroy/Istockphoto, p. 9; John Prudence/Istockphoto, p. 12; Piotr Przeszlo/Istockphoto, p.
13 (middle); Jordan Shaw/Istockphoto, pp. 1, 23 (bottom); Jamie Wilson/Istockphoto, p. 14;
Claire Francis/MEA Photos, p. 10; Rachel Weill/Photolibrary, p. 20 (top); Photos.com, pp. 5, 13
(bottom).

While every care has been taken to trace and acknowledge copyright, the publisher tenders
their apologies for any accidental infringement where copyright has proved untraceable.
Where the attempt has been unsuccessful, the publisher welcomes information that would
redress the situation.

Please note
At the time of printing, the Internet addresses appearing in this book were correct.
Owing to the dynamic nature of the Internet, however, we cannot guarantee that all these
addresses will remain correct.

Contents

Recreational sports   4

Where to fish   6

Getting started   10

Fishing gear   12

Setting up your gear   14

Casting   18

Finding fish   20

Hooking a fish   22

Landing a fish   24

Releasing a fish   26

Fishing around the world   28

Interview: Fishing crazy!   30

Glossary   31

Index   32

Glossary words

When a word is printed in **bold**, you can look up its meaning in the Glossary on page 31.

Recreational sports

Recreational sports are the activities we do in our spare time. These are sports that people do for fun, not necessarily for competition.

You have probably tried some recreational sports already. Maybe you would like to know more about them, or to find out about new ones? Try as many as you can – not just fishing. Also try biking, hiking, kayaking, climbing and snorkelling. This will help you to find one you really love doing.

Benefits of sport

Recreational sports give people lots of pleasure, but they also have other benefits. People who exercise regularly usually have better health. They find it easier to concentrate, and do better at school or at work.

'The two best times to fish are when it's raining and when it ain't.'
Patrick F. McManus, fishing writer

Fishing often takes place in beautiful surroundings.

Fishing

Hooking your first fish is a great thrill. When the fishing line goes tight, and then zips through the water, it can be very exciting. Today, millions of people around the world are hooked on the thrill of fishing.

There are lots of places to try fishing. You might start at your local **dam**, and then end up fishing great rivers and oceans. Almost anywhere there is water, there will probably be an **angler** trying to catch a fish.

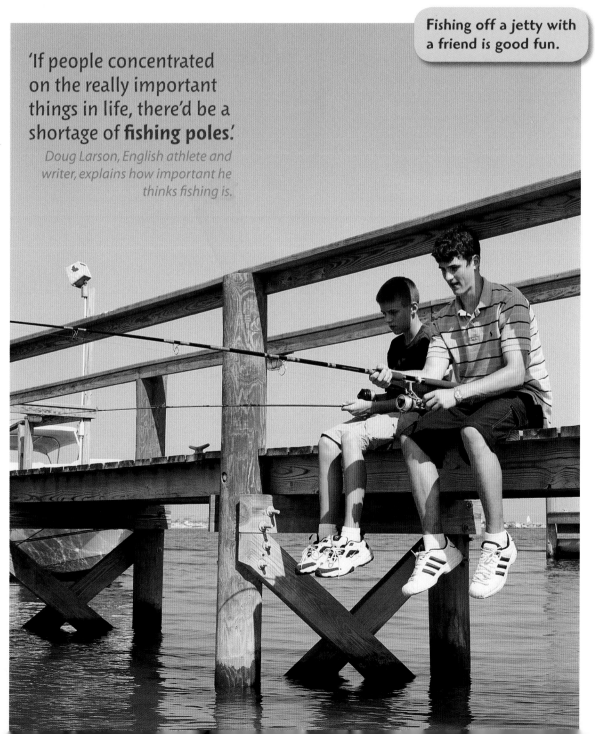

'If people concentrated on the really important things in life, there'd be a shortage of **fishing poles**.'
Doug Larson, English athlete and writer, explains how important he thinks fishing is.

Fishing off a jetty with a friend is good fun.

Where to fish

There are lots of great places to fish. If you live near the coast, you will probably start fishing in the sea. If you live inland, you probably fish in creeks and dams.

Piers and jetties

Almost every town near the coast has a pier or jetty. Fish often gather near them looking for food or shelter. This makes them great places to fish. All you have to do is drop in a hook and line with some tasty bait, and hope for a bite.

WATCH OUT!

People sometimes fish from rocks at the water's edge. This can be very dangerous, because of the risk of being swept away by waves.

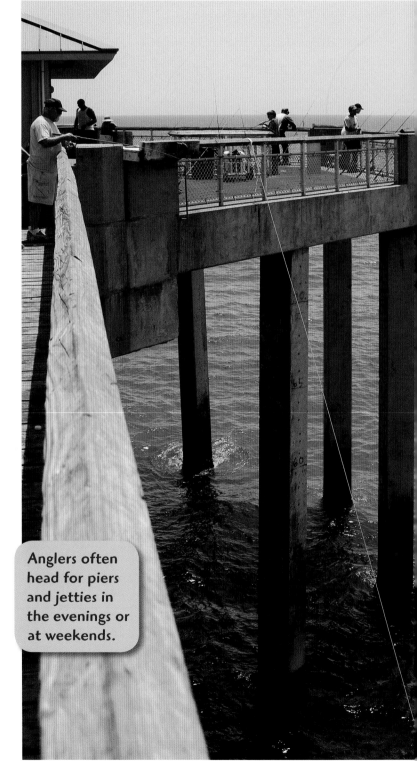

Anglers often head for piers and jetties in the evenings or at weekends.

Fish looking for food in the surf may bite your bait instead.

Surf beaches

Surf **casting** is fishing from the beach, casting your line out into the surf. Fish feed in the churned-up water near the shore. With a bit of luck, one will mistake your bait for its proper food. The equipment is similar to other fishing gear, but most people use longer rods for surf casting.

WATCH OUT!

Always wear a life jacket when fishing from a boat, in case you fall in.

Boats

Fishing in a boat means you can fish in areas you could not otherwise reach. A boat can take you out into the harbour, into an **estuary** or even to offshore islands. Almost anywhere you think the fish might be biting, the boat can take you. Boat anglers use similar equipment to the kind used fishing from a pier.

A boat can help you to catch fish you would not find inland.

Tidal areas

Tidal areas along the banks of rivers near the sea are good places to fish. In hot countries these areas have mangrove forests growing along the water's edge. Mangroves have tangled roots that are underwater at high tide. Smaller fish love to shelter in the roots. Bigger fish come to eat the smaller fish, and anglers come to catch the bigger fish. Mangrove fishing is almost impossible, and dangerous, from the shore. It is great fun from a boat.

Rivers

Rivers are great places to fish. Study the river for a place where the fish might be feeding. Then cast your line and see if you can get a bite.

WATCH OUT!

Always get permission if you have to cross private property to get to your fishing spot.

Tidal areas are home to many different kinds of fish.

Dams and lakes

One of the most popular places for fishing is on dams. Here you can fish from the shore, from piers or jetties, or from a boat. Dams often have fish put in them specially for anglers to catch.

Small lakes can be great for fishing, too. There are lots of different kinds of lake fishing, but the same rod you use for sea fishing will be fine on a lake, too.

'Even a fish wouldn't get into trouble if he kept his mouth shut.'

Author unknown. Part of the trick of fishing is working out how to get the fish to open its mouth and bite your hook.

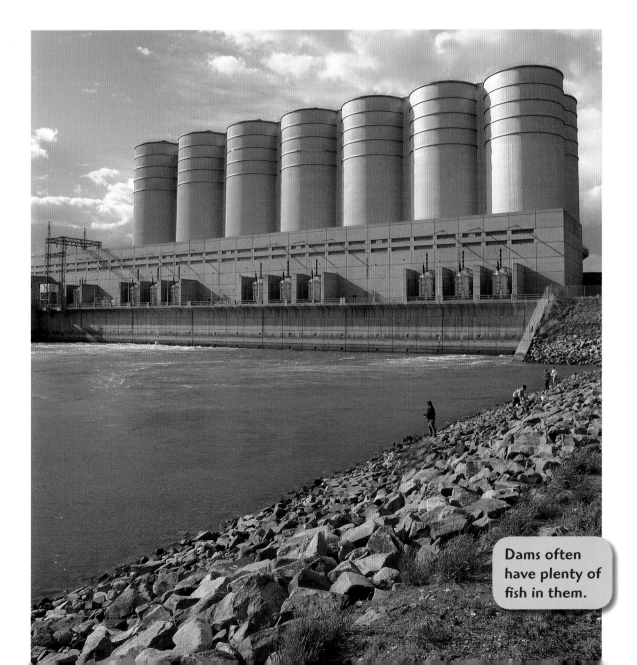

Dams often have plenty of fish in them.

Getting started

Handlines are an easy, cheap way to start fishing.
A handline is a fishing line that you feed out and pull in by hand.

Rigging a handline

The line on a handline is tied to the reel, then wound around it.
The handle can be specially designed, or just a thick stick. A simple
way to rig your handline is to tie a sinker at the end. Using another
piece of line, tie the hook a bit further up.

When you lower the sinker into the water, it weighs the line
straight down. The hook and bait hang higher up. Set the hook so that
it dangles about ten centimetres above the sinker. This arrangement
is good for fishing from a boat or pier.

A typical handline
like this is suitable for
fishing from jetties,
piers or boats.

Fishing from a boat, jetty or pier

Handlines can be used for casting out from a boat, jetty or pier. Casting a handline takes a bit of practice.

Technique

Casting a handline

This technique has been used around the world for thousands of years. You can use it for almost any kind of fishing. Always check there is no one nearby who could get hooked on your line.

1 If you are right-handed, hold the handle in your left hand.

2 Hold the line in your right hand, about 1–2 metres from the end.

3 Face the direction you want to cast. Twirl the line around like a lasso. Let it go.

4 Let the line run off the handle freely, then stop it when the bait hits the water.

Fishing gear

Fishing gear is called tackle. This is the equipment you use to catch fish and carry it home. Tackle includes a rod, reel, line, hooks, spinners, lures, sinkers and a bucket.

Picking a rod and reel

There are many different rods and reels. To get started, tackle you can use for lots of different types of fishing is best. Ask local anglers questions to find out what tackle is best for your area.

- What kind of fish do people usually catch around here?
- What kind of tackle is best for catching them?

Many people start fishing with a rod and reel that can be used from piers, boats and other areas where only a short cast is needed. A 2-metre rod that can hold a fish weighing up to 8 kilograms, plus a simple fixed spool reel, should be fine.

rod

fishing line

lure

hook

reel attaches to rod here

spool holds line

adjustable brake

bale arm

reel lever, for winding in line

A short rod with a fixed spool reel is good for beginners.

Terminal tackle

Terminal tackle is the equipment that goes on the end of your line. The tackle is attached to the trace, which is a finer piece of line attached to the fishing line. If a large fish breaks your line, only the trace will break . You can set this up in the same way as for handline fishing, but there are also lots of other ways. The three main set-ups are:

- with a hook at the end of the line, and a sinker further up to keep the line deep in the water. Sometimes there is a swivel between the sinker and the hook, to keep the line from tangling.

- with a **float** further up the line. The rest of the tackle dangles from the float.

- with a **spinner**, or lure, tied to the end of the line. These are designed to look like bait, so when you reel them in, fish are tempted to bite them. Only then do they discover your lure has a hook attached.

lure

sinkers

hook and sinker

floats

spinner

Different kinds of terminal tackle can be used in many combinations to catch different kinds of fish.

Setting up your gear

Once you have got your first fishing tackle, you will need to set it up. Put your rod together, add line to the reel and add the terminal tackle. You are ready to fish!

Putting your rod together

Most rods are simple to put together. They mostly come in two pieces, and one piece pushes inside the other. The place where it fits together is called the joint. When the joints have been pushed together, you have a fishing rod.

The fishing line runs through little loops, called eyelets, on the rod. When you push the rod together, make sure these all line up with the reel. That way, your fishing line will run in and out easily.

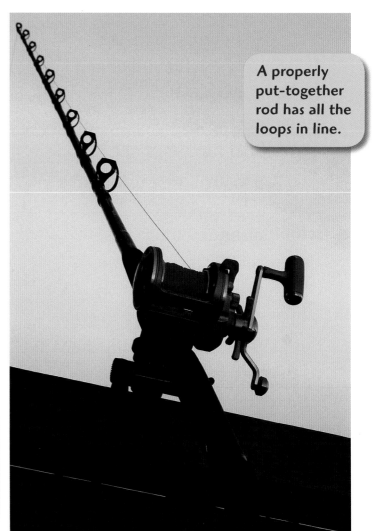

A properly put-together rod has all the loops in line.

Top tip!

If the joints on your rod are loose, rub the inside part with candle wax.

Adding line to your reel

Many new reels come with line already attached. Even so, one day your line will snap or be damaged and need replacing. New line comes on a plastic spool. You need to wind it onto your reel.

Technique

Winding line onto a reel

Adding line to a reel correctly will mean that the line will feed properly when you cast.

1 Pull back the bale arm on the reel. Tie the end of the line to the reel using a double slip knot.

2 Close the bale arm and gently wind in the line. It helps if someone else holds the spool.

3 The line should be added evenly. Do not completely fill the reel. If you fill it to the edges, the line can fall off and tangle.

Tying your hooks to the end of the line

There are lots of knots for tying a hook to the end of your fishing line. One of the best is the tucked half-blood knot.

Top tip!

Wet your knots before pulling on them. This helps the knot to stay tight.

Technique

Tucked half-blood knot

1 Pass about 30 centimetres of line through the **eye** of the hook.

2 Loop the end of the line back over itself at least six times.

3 Bring the end of the line up through the first loop you made, then down through the big loop running from one end of the knot to the other.

4 Pull the knot lightly, wet it, then tighten it fully and trim excess line.

Adding a hook to the line

Sometimes hooks are tied further up the line. You might have a sinker at the end of the line, and need to add a hook further up. A good knot for this is the stand-off loop knot.

Technique:

Stand-off loop knot

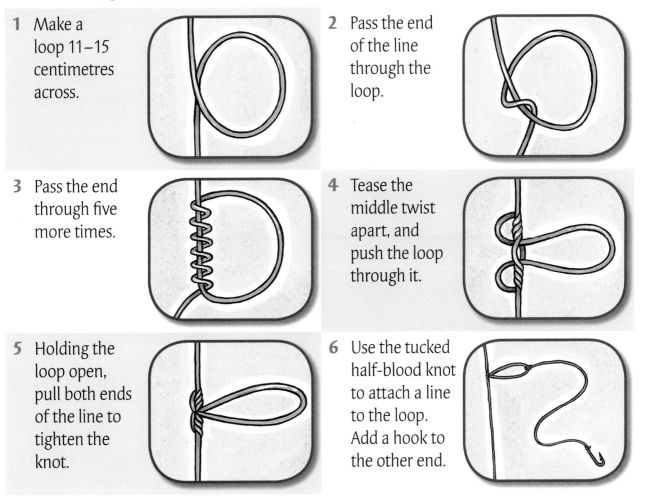

1 Make a loop 11–15 centimetres across.

2 Pass the end of the line through the loop.

3 Pass the end through five more times.

4 Tease the middle twist apart, and push the loop through it.

5 Holding the loop open, pull both ends of the line to tighten the knot.

6 Use the tucked half-blood knot to attach a line to the loop. Add a hook to the other end.

Sinkers and floats

Sinkers and floats do just the jobs it sounds like. Sinkers are designed to make your fishing line sink. Floats are designed to keep the hook floating at a set depth. Both come in lots of different shapes and sizes. Some have a little hoop on the end for tying on your line. Others have a hole through the middle, which the line goes through.

Casting

Casting is the technique of throwing your bait out into the water. It is important to know how to cast accurately, to get your bait to where the fish are feeding.

The long rods used for surf fishing can cast over 100 metres.

Basic casting

The simplest cast is the overhead cast. This cast can be used for all sorts of fishing, from piers, boats and the shore. Before casting, check that there is nothing your line can get caught in, such as trees or power lines. If there are things in the way, cast at another spot.

Practising casting

Practise your casting in non-fishing areas. When you do go fishing, you will be ready to cast to the right spot, straight away.

Top tip!

Although you can cast a handline, a rod and reel helps you to cast much further.

Technique

Overhead cast

1 Let out a little line from the reel. Aim for the end of the line to come about two-thirds of the way down the rod.

2 Open the bale arm on the reel. Hold the line against the rod. This will stop it running out before you are ready to cast.

3 Check behind you to make sure no one is in the way. Take the rod back over your head and behind you. Tilt the rod sideways slightly, so that the hook does not get caught up in the rod.

4 Whip the rod forward. As the hook flies past the rod tip, lift your finger off the line. This will let the line go whizzing out.

5 As the hook hits the water, put your finger on the spool. When the line stops running off the reel, flip the bale arm closed.

6 Wait a few moments, then reel in a few turns. This will take up any slack line.

Finding fish

There are a few tricks to finding fish. If you can work out where the fish are likely to be feeding, and what they are feeding on, it will help you catch them.

Choosing your bait

Choose bait that will seem tasty to the fish you are trying to catch. Bass eat worms from the seabed, or pieces of crab. If you bait your hook with sea worms or crab, you have a good chance of catching bass.

This hook is being baited with live bait to attract larger fish, who feed on them.

Piers and jetties

Piers and jetties are good places to find fish. These places provide fish with food and shelter. Prawns, crabs and other small sea creatures live under piers and jetties. Larger fish feed on the small sea creatures. The larger fish are a good catch for an angler who has chosen just the right bait.

Jetties are home to lots of fish.

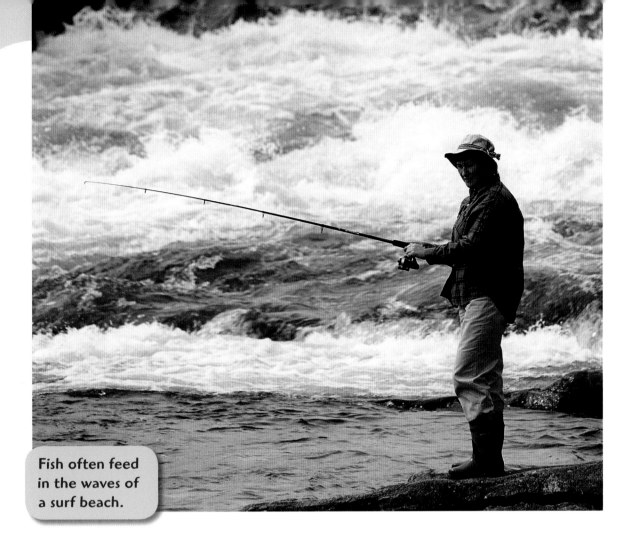

Fish often feed in the waves of a surf beach.

Surf beaches

Waves coming into a surf beach disturb the small creatures that fish eat. Casting out beyond the third **breaker** often reaches an area where fish are feeding. You may also find fish feeding beside a rocky area. The surf disturbs creatures living on the rocks, and these are then eaten by fish.

Dams

Dams have lots of places where fish like to feed. The edges of the dam are often best. Try to find a spot where fish might shelter or feed. These include:
- shady areas
- near bridge pylons
- near dam walls.

Top tip!

Fish are often easier to catch from a surf beach when the tide is coming in.

Hooking a fish

The most exciting moment in fishing is when you know you have hooked a fish. When this happens, there are a few tricks that will help you get the fish to shore.

Setting the hook

Setting the hook ensures that the fish is properly hooked. When you think you have a bite, give your rod a firm upward movement. This will cause the hook to set, or sink into the fish's mouth. Now the fish will not be able to swim off. Try to keep the line tight once the fish is on the hook.

Using the rod

If a fish pulls strongly on the line, you can use the rod to help reel it in. Hold the rod up high, almost straight up in the air. The rod will bend towards the fish, taking some of the strain. Lower the rod and wind the reel, then lift the rod up again to pull the fish in. If you have caught a big one, this makes your line less likely to break.

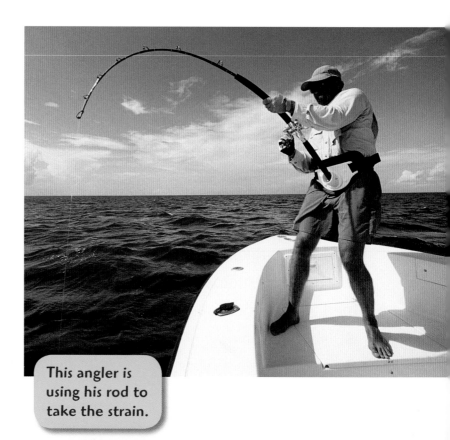

This angler is using his rod to take the strain.

Fighting fish

Fish that try especially hard to escape when they are hooked are known as fighting fish, or game fish. Fighting fish are the hardest, and most fun, to hook. They often take the bait very suddenly, unlike other fish, which nibble on the bait.

Some fish actually leap out of the water when they are hooked.

Technique

Hooking a fighting fish

Use these tips to help you hook a fish that fights against being caught.

1 When you set the hook, the line will begin to zip off your reel. The fish is running. Let it go. Keep your rod held high.
2 If the fish heads for a place where your line could get snagged, steer it away by pulling it sideways.
3 Once the fish slows down, gently begin to reel it towards you. Be ready for the fish to run again. If it does, let it go.
4 Repeat the process until the fish can be brought right in near you.

'The fishing was good. It was the catching that was bad.'

A.K. Best, well-known angler.

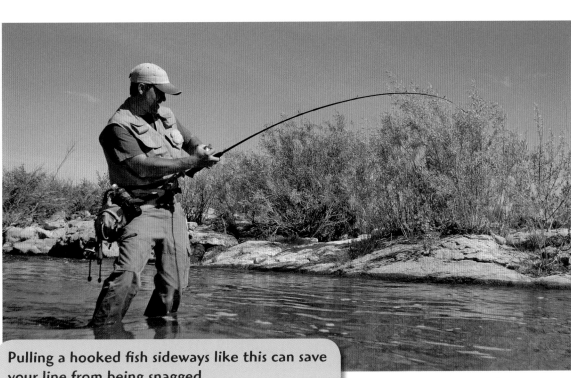

Pulling a hooked fish sideways like this can save your line from being snagged.

Landing a fish

Once you have got a fish reeled in, you still have to get it ashore. This is called landing a fish. It can be a tricky thing to manage.

Using a landing net

A landing net is a special net with a long handle. Boat and shore anglers use them to land fish.

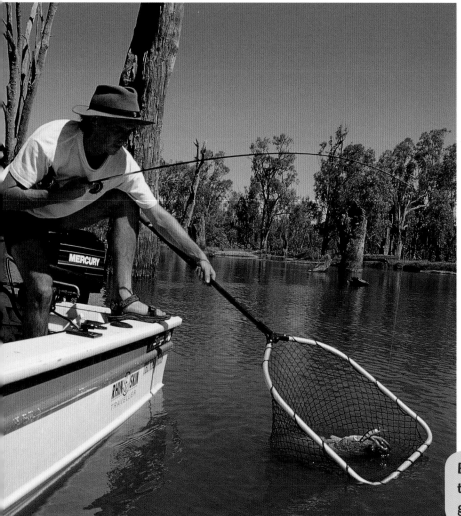

Technique

Using a landing net

Always have your landing net within reach. That way, you will be able to get hold of it easily.

1 Bring the fish in as close as possible.
2 Slip the net into the water behind the fish, so you do not frighten it.
3 Lift your rod to guide the fish into the net.
4 Once the fish is in the net, lift it out of the water.

Bring your fish to the landing net as gently as possible.

Pier and jetty fishing

There is really only one way to land a fish if you are on a pier or jetty. Reel it gently up from the water. Then, swing it in and lie it on the deck.

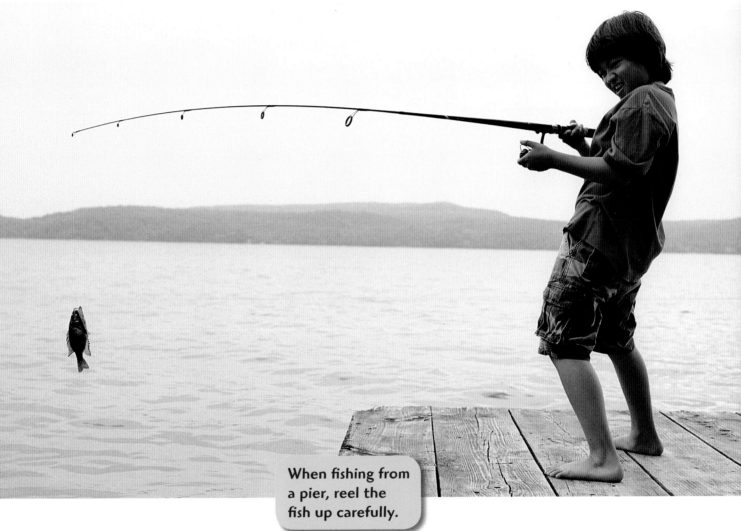

When fishing from a pier, reel the fish up carefully.

Hook removal

Once the fish has been landed, you need to remove the hook. Never put your fingers inside a fish's mouth. They have very powerful jaws. If the hook is deep inside its mouth, use a disgorger. These can be bought in any tackle shop.

'It is not a fish until it's on the bank.'

Irish Proverb.

Releasing a fish

Some anglers let fish go after catching them. This is called catch and release.

Why release fish?

You may decide to release a fish for several reasons:

- The fish is too small to be kept.
- It might be a kind of fish that you are not allowed to catch.
- There may be limits on how many fish you are allowed. These are called bag limits.
- It might be an **inedible** fish.
- You might decide that catching the fish is what you enjoy, but you may not want to eat it.

Top tip!

If possible, release fish into cool, deep water. This gives them a better chance of surviving.

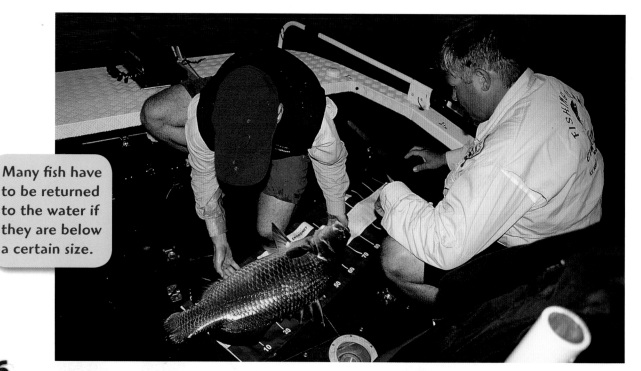

Many fish have to be returned to the water if they are below a certain size.

26

Releasing a fish

If you plan to release a fish, try to land it as quickly as possible.
This way, the fish will not get so tired that it cannot swim off later.

Releasing a fish

Follow these tips to release a fish without hurting it:

1. Use barbless hooks. These are hooks without notches on the end. These are easier to remove.
2. If you can, remove the hook and release the fish while it is still in the water.
3. If you do remove the fish from the water, use wet hands or a wet towel to hold it gently.
4. Try not to use a net.
5. Remove the hook as quickly as possible. If the hook is deep inside the fish, cut the line close to the fish's mouth. The juices in its stomach will eventually dissolve the hook.

If the fish does not swim away after a second or two, slide it gently back and forth in the water to help it recover.

Fishing around the world

Almost anywhere there is water there will be anglers. These are just a few of the best fishing spots in the world.

Salmon and trout fishing

Name Scottish Highlands
Location United Kingdom
Description Probably the most famous salmon and trout-fishing area in the world, in beautiful (if often rainy) scenery.

Fighting fish

Name Southern India
Location India
Description Southern India is home to the mahseer, a giant fish that can weigh over 50 kilograms. Mahseer are famous for the way they fight against being landed.

Salmon fishing

Name Pacific North-west

Location United States/ Canada

Description The north-west corner of North America is famous for its salmon fishing. When the fish swim up the river to breed, anglers have to watch out for bears standing in the water looking for fish.

Reefs, rivers or mangroves

Name Queensland

Location Australia

Description Queensland has almost everything an angler could want. You can boat fish the offshore reefs or coastal mangroves, or head for the region's rivers.

Trout and salmon fishing

Name Lago Nahuel Huapi

Location Argentina

Description The Patagonia region is among the world's most beautiful fishing areas. Trout and salmon were introduced from Europe a hundred years ago, and now live in many rivers and lakes.

Interview: Fishing crazy!

Dave has been fishing since he was nine years old. He now works in a fishing tackle shop, as well as guiding tourists to good fishing spots.

How did you get into fishing?

My mates and I got handlines that we used to dangle off the pier. We caught more crabs than fish, but we used to go down there most weekends. It just grew from there, really. As soon as we could afford to we bought ourselves rods and tackle, and started fishing in different places.

What is your favourite kind of fishing?

My friend Andy's dad had a boat. He'd take us out once in a while, and we'd go into the mangroves and spin for mangrove jacks. They fight so hard that I think they're my favourites.

Any advice for young anglers?

Well, I've spent a lot of money on tackle I didn't really need. Expensive tackle doesn't always help you catch more fish. It's better to learn about the eating habits of the fish in your area, and the tides. That way you'll put your bait in the right bit of water at the right time!

What are the best places to find out more about fishing?

Most libraries have good books on fishing. Local tackle shops usually have information about bag limits and other restrictions. The Internet is also a good place to find information about what's been being caught in your area.

Glossary

angler

a person who goes fishing for fun, normally using a hook, line and rod

breaker

a breaking wave

casting

throwing your line and bait onto the water in whichever direction you choose, usually using a rod

dam

large wall that blocks the flow of a river – water from the river builds up behind the dam, making a lake

estuary

area at the mouth of a river, where the water is salty sea water as well as fresh water

eye

the small hole at the top of a sinker, hook or float, which a fishing line can be tied to

fishing pole

another word for a fishing rod

float

fishing equipment which keeps the hook dangling at a certain height

inedible

something that cannot be eaten, perhaps because it is poisonous or tastes bad

spinner

spoon-shaped disc with a hook beside it, which tricks fish into thinking it is a little, silvery fish when reeled in

tidal areas

areas where land is uncovered as the tide falls and covered up by the water as the tide rises again

Index

A

adding line to reel   15
angler   5, 6, 7, 9, 12, 22, 24

B

bag limits   26, 30
bait   6, 7, 10, 11, 13, 18, 20, 23
bale arm   12, 15, 19
bass   20
benefits of sport   4
boat fishing   7, 8, 9, 10, 11, 12, 18, 24, 29
bucket   12

C

casting   11, 18–19
creeks   6

D

dams   5, 6, 9, 21
disgorger   25

E

equipment   14–17
exercise   4
eye   16
eyelet   14

F

fighting fish   23, 28
fishing spots   20–21, 28–9, 30
fixed spool reel   12
float   13, 17

H

handlines   10, 11, 13, 18, 30
hook   6, 10, 12, 13, 16, 17, 19, 20, 22, 25, 27
hook removal   25, 27

J

jetty and pier fishing   6, 9, 10, 11, 12, 18, 20, 25, 30

K

knots   16, 17

L

landing net   24
life jacket   7
line   5, 6, 11, 12, 13, 14, 15, 16, 17, 18, 19, 22, 23, 27
lure   12, 13

M

mangroves jacks   30
mangroves   8, 29, 30

O

overhead cast   18, 19

R

reel   12, 14, 15, 18, 19, 22, 23
releasing fish   26–27
rivers   5, 8, 29
rod   6, 7, 9, 12, 14, 18, 19, 22, 23, 24, 30
rod technique   22, 23

S

salmon   28–9
setting the hook   22, 23
shore fishing   6, 9, 11, 18, 24
sinker   10, 13, 17
spinner   12, 13
spool   12, 15, 19
stand-off loop knot   17
surf fishing   7, 18, 21

T

tackle   12, 13, 14, 25, 30
terminal tackle   13, 14
trace   13
trout   28–9
tucked half-blood knot   16